Can These Bones Live?

Hope, Help, & Strength
for Interdependent Relationships

Can These Bones Live?

Hope, Help, & Strength
for Interdependent Relationships

Ricky Allen

Copyright

Copyright © 2017 **Ricky Allen**. All rights reserved. This book or any portion thereof may not be reproduced or used in any manner whatsoever without the express written permission of **Ricky Allen** except for the use of brief quotations in a book review.

Printed in the United States of America

First Printing,

Second edition:

ISBN-13: 978-1-947656-03-1

ISBN10: 1947656031

The Butterfly Typeface Publishing
PO BOX 56193
Little Rock Arkansas 72215
www.butterflytypeface.com
butterflytypeface.imw@gmail.com

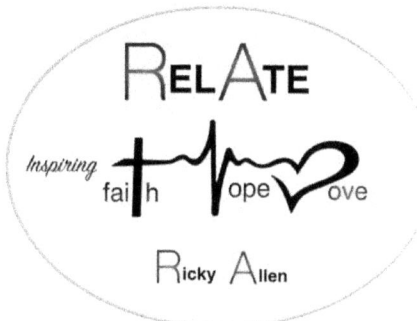

Mission

The mission of RELATE is to inspire faith, hope and love through biblical precepts and examples in order to realize and maximize purposeful interdependent relationships.

Vision

Learning, Living and Leaving Legacies!

Meaningful relationships are one of life's greatest resources. The manner in which we build them is among life's greatest legacies. *Can These Bones Live* is a powerful and practical guide to restoring Hope, Help, & Strength to Interdependent Relationships.

Dedication

I joyfully dedicate this book to my family.

I am eternally grateful for the time and space we have to discover the joys and sorrows of sharing our lives and the power to decide which will be our companions.

Sensations of My Heart – Awaken

Years have passed… such a brief moment in time.

Awakened from my deep sleep!

Life's journey has been long… its lessons hard.

Awakened to greater discovery!

More pieces added to the puzzle… another mystery unveiled.

Awakened to unlimited creativity!

It's another chapter… a story that only my life can tell.

Awaken to live more abundantly!

Table of Contents

Preface 19
Introduction 23
Chapter One 27
Choices 28
    Choosing Your Master 30
    Choosing Your Mission 35
    Choosing Your Companion 37
Chapter Two 41
Connect 42
    Competition in the Social Arena 43
    Competition in the Sacred Arena 44
    Storming 51
    Proactive Engagement 52
    Reactive Engagement 52
    Proactive Disengagement 53
Chapter Three 55
Where Are The B-O-N-E-S? 56
    Blessings 56
    Oneness 58
    Nurturing 60
    Edifying 62
    Sacrifice 63
Chapter Four 65

Bone of My Bone 66
    Destruction of Myth(s) 67
    A Message to the Man 72
    A Message to the Woman 73
Chapter Five 77
Reconciling Differences 78
    Peace Faking 78
    Peace Breaking 79
Chapter Six 93
Maintaining Interdependent Relationships 94
    Communication 94
    Passion 96
    Intimacy 97
About the Author 107
Acclaim for 'Can These Bones Live?' 109

Foreword

Have you ever stopped to think about how the relationships we enter into as adults are impacted by the relationship experiences of our youth? Often it is our parents, siblings, and friends who model for us the types of relationships we will have as adults.

Author Ricky Allen has given this idea a lot of thought. While his initial desire to write about this phenomenon was to sort through his own anguish, he quickly understood that he was indeed required to *teach* what he had *learned*.

The complicated thing about life-help books is that they can often come off as *preachy* and impersonal. I'm sure it is because the author has chosen to 'keep themselves out of it' and focus on their audience. After all, we have been conditioned to believe that the journey we are experiencing has nothing to do with us. That is true to an extent, especially while we are in the vortex of the storm. However, as authors we understand that stories are how we connect and identify with each other. While our journeys begin as a method of self-healing, we must be willing to divulge the route we chose in order to make our readers feel secure. We must validate ourselves by being *in the story*.

So, why should you listen to what Ricky Allen has to say about interdependent relationships? Well, he does have the professional credentials (Corporate Trainer in Organizational Effectives and Process Improvements for a Fortune 500 Company, motivational speaker, spiritual leader etc.) to speak on such things. However, what gives his book, "Can These Bones Live?" weight is not his professional accomplishments, but rather his personal failures. Ricky Allen can relate to an inappropriate encounter, a broken marriage, a failed friendship, a strained sibling connection, a missing parent, and the ensuing heartbreak and shame of it all. What further qualifies him to write about these broken relationships, in my opinion, is his commitment to telling the truth no matter how painful it may be.

The technical aspects of this book are thought-provoking. You will find yourself reading the same sentence more than once, not because you don't comprehend, but rather because the concept is so profound. The *ah-ha* moments are plenty!

This composer of lyrical literature has a mesmerizing way of poetically penning words so that they appear to leap off the page and into the wounded heart of the reader.

Author Ricky Allen, a very composed, organized, and thoughtful writer, has managed to weave the smartness of a *life-help* book, with an often mesmerizing take on a memoir, together with an added pinch of poetry into a literary work of art!

Interdependent relationships affect all of us in some fashion, so undoubtedly you will find yourself between the pages of this manuscript. This book and its accompanying journal are not only to be read, but to be experienced and practiced. Prepare to acknowledge and release past hurts and grasp the lifeline offered through this exquisite *literary goodness*.

The truth about mending relationships is that the process begins with pointing the guilty finger at yourself. That can be intimidating to say the least. However, I challenge you to push past the comfortability of it as Ricky did. What you discover will not only free you from your past, but it can propel you into a happier and more satisfied existence.

"Can These Bones Live?" will give you 'life' by offering hope to what can feel like a hopeless situation.

Iris M. Williams
"God Is in The Details"

Preface

A tree will never be a tree again once cut down. Ask, what can I make from the sawdust on the ground?

There I was limping through life, unknowingly dragging my brokenness from one relationship to another while looking for someone to make it better. After experiencing multiple divorces within a 10-year period, I stood looking at the residue. It was too much to make sense of all at one time. I was certain that these relationships didn't end due to the lack of love or value for the institute of marriage. Therefore, I had to continue peeling the layers back. Finally, I got to that point where I asked 'why' for the last time. The answer was striking to me. It caused me to confront the pains of my past. It was the lingering effects of dysfunction in primary interdependent relationships. Good intentions don't guarantee good results. The effects of childhood abandonment, neglect, and abuse were manifesting itself in reserved ways.

Embarrassed by these life experiences, I cried out. "Lord! What do I do now? This wasn't supposed to happen to me. After all, I'm a Christian. Not only that, *you* called me to serve in Pastoral ministry."

Lovingly, He said to me, "I didn't call you based on your situation. My plans for you have not changed. I want you to become better, not bitter. You are not alone."

Has "it" happened to you? Are you experiencing some brokenness due to dysfunctional interdependent relationships be it among family, friends, or even in the workplace? Have you given up on being fulfilled while sharing time and space with another? Do you repeatedly find yourself in toxic relationships? Allow me to speak to you! Hope, Help, and Strength are within your grasp!

As a way of coping with my relationship dysfunctions, I found that writing poetry was somewhat a release. It afforded me an outlet for self-expressions without the feelings of quilt or judgement. Until now, I've been very selective in sharing my poetry with others. Reminiscent of my childhood, my poetry exposes the guarded "Sensations of My Heart". I have chosen to share a few of those sensations with you as you read.

Sensations of My Heart -- When it happens to you

When it doesn't work regardless to how hard you try.

Ask, do I learn from this and live, or live just to die.

A tree will never be a tree again once cut down.

Ask, what can I make from the sawdust on the ground.

Countless rehearsals of "why" are like spinning wheels that create ruts.

You've got to do something different to get different results.

Becoming better and not bitter can be the greatest test.

You can face it with courage when you've given it your best.

Can These Bones Live? is a powerful and practical guide to restoring Hope, Help, & Strength to Interdependent Relationships. The content herein is meant for those seeking fulfilling and trustworthy interdependent relationships.

Read it! Embrace it! It will refresh your spirit, refocus your will, and restore your soul!

Introduction

Son of Man, Can These Bones Live?

Interdependent relationships are the ways in which two or more people are dependent on one another in order to connect the full gamut of human existence. Simply put, "It's the independent (or separate) contributions of two or more parts to uniquely create one whole, purposeful, and functional unit." Each part functions in the best interest of the other.

God's life plan for the human race is not independence. Neither is it codependence. His life plan is interdependence that reflects His unselfish love for His creation and His commitment to its good. He intends for relationships to be whole, purposeful, and fulfilling.

Can These Bones Live?

Purposeful interdependent relationships don't *naturally* disintegrate. The contributing factors are abandonment, neglect, and abuse.

- Abandonment: To Withdraw From
- Neglect: Present But Remiss in Caring For
- Abuse: To Improperly Use

Howbeit, emotional, spiritual or physical (See Workbook), the effect of these contributing factors can follow you a lifetime if not confronted and result in frail interdependent relationships.

We see constant assault within interdependent relationships rather than peaceful resolutions. Homes, churches, and schools, which are our greatest institutions of learning, have become war grounds rather than safe havens. The pursuit of happiness has been confused with the fulfillment of purpose.

This condition reminds me of the alienated relationship between the Israelites and The Lord God (Ezekiel 36, 37). The Israelites abandoned their Sovereign God's instructions, neglected one another,

Can These Bones Live?

and abused their privileges. They operated in illegitimate authority. Consequently, they ended up in Babylonian captivity. They forfeited their rights to fulfillment which could only come from proper function within their interdependent relationship with their Sovereign God. They were like a valley of lifeless dry bones.

God transported the prophet, Ezekiel (The Watchman), by the Spirit, to a valley full of bones (Ezekiel 37:1-3). There he noticed that the bones were very dry, bleached, and baked under the hot sun. God asked the prophet a notable question: "Son of man, can these bones live?" Was there potential for life in these lifeless frames? Ezekiel knew that humanly speaking, it was impossible, so his answer was somewhat guarded. He realized that only the Sovereign Lord knew the answer.

I experienced this dilemma (an alienated relationship) early in life. I grew up loving a father I never had. I was alienated from my father due to my parents divorcing shortly after I was born. I knew who my father was; however, I didn't have a purposeful interdependent relationship with him. As if that wasn't enough, the man in our home was an alcoholic and abusive. Moreover, there were those who pretended to be friends of the family while all along inappropriately exploiting my youthful innocence, which confused my desire to be accepted and protected. I didn't share this experience with anyone. Consequently, I grew up feeling disconnected and insecure. I longed for validation.

It was my valley of dry bones.

Can These Bones Live?

Chapter One

CHOICES

A misdirected decision in any of these areas can lead to a misdirected and empty life.

Can These Bones Live?

Choices

Sometimes, choices are made for us. Inadvertently, we are left with the muddled task of cleaning up such choices.

Life is full of choices. Each day we are faced with making decisions that will somehow affect the balance of our day and perhaps our entire lives. Some are routine and some not so routine. Have you ever made a wrong choice and tried to make it right by making that wrong choice a permanent choice? This might seem like a brain teaser; however, it isn't. It's a reality check.

Perhaps, three of the most important life choices are:

- ☐ Who is your Master?
- ☐ What is your Mission?
- ☐ Who are your Companions?

Can These Bones Live?

You have the freedom of choice; however, a misdirected decision in any of these areas can lead to a misdirected and empty life.

"Enter ye in at the strait gate: for wide is the gate, and broad is the way, that leadeth to destruction, and many there be which go in there at: Because strait is the gate, and narrow is the way, which leadeth unto life, and few there be that find it" (Matthew 7:13-14 KJV).

This scripture represents the freedom of choice as well as the importance of making knowledgeable choices.

Broad is the easiest and most popular way. Just because the majority seems to embrace an idea or norm doesn't make it right. The end could lead to destruction of values, principles, integrity, and purposeful interdependent relationships.

Narrow is the way that leads to life. Few discover the fulfilling life offered in the straight and narrow way. The challenge here is not to conform; rather, be transformed by renewing the mind daily.

Can These Bones Live?

Choosing Your Master

I vividly remember this defining moment in my life. I was an honor student, an all-star baseball player, and a varsity basketball player; however, I had an inward emptiness that would not go away. The adventures I had chosen led to superficial happiness. The day came when I realized that I didn't like what I had become. I was sixteen-years-old and popular but misdirected and living without true purpose. I was on a quiet path of destruction.

One day a couple of high school classmates came to me and began sharing the love of Christ. They began sharing ways I could respond to His love; the first way was by accepting Him as my Savior. My reply to their words was that the temptations in my life were too enticing and too strong. They then directed me to a scripture found in **I Corinthians 10:13**. This scripture let me know that temptation was common and that God loved me so much and would not allow Satan to tempt me with more than I could endure. It also assured me that God would make provisions for me to escape temptation. At that point, the Word of God erased my excuses for not choosing Christ as my Savior and Lord.

The time came, and I had to make a choice! I needed direction! I needed purpose! On a cold Tuesday night, January 1980, I left a basketball game at half time to attend a revival. As the minister shared the Word of God, I felt life coming to my spiritually dead condition. It was a burning truth that opened my heart to the love God had for me and revived my spirit.

I would like to share the power of those words with you from the Message Bible in Contemporary Language.

"With the arrival of Jesus, the Messiah, that fateful dilemma is resolved. Those who enter into Christ's being-here-for-us no longer have to live under a continuous, low-lying black cloud. A new power is in operation. The Spirit of life in Christ, like a strong wind, has magnificently cleared the air, freeing you from a fated lifetime of brutal tyranny at the hands of sin and death" (Romans 8:1-2 MSG).

Can These Bones Live?

From such penetrating truth, I realized:

A purposeful interdependent relationship with God was my greatest need. I could never be strong enough to resist the lust of my flesh, the lust of my eyes, and the pride in my life without God's Spirit regenerating my mind and heart.

I also realized that God's grace was sufficient for me. I didn't have to live under the dark cloud of my past. In Him, I had a heritage and a bright future.

I then accepted responsibility and chose to commit my life to the Lordship of Jesus Christ. Life literally took on a new meaning and a new direction for me.

My "Bones" began to live!

You might ask, "What does this have to do with interdependent relationships" or "What does this have to do with me"? My answer… everything.

The most important interdependent relationship you can have is your relationship with God, The Heavenly Father and The Ruler of Heaven and Earth.

"Live in me. Make your home in me just as I do in you. In the same way that a branch can't bear grapes by itself but only by being joined to the vine, you can't bear fruit unless you are joined with me"(John 15:4 MSG).

When you choose to make Christ your Master, you choose to live a harmonious adventure with God. Jesus Christ embodies Interdependence. He mediates our relationship with The Heavenly Father, as well as with others. He provides:

- ☐ A Common Bond (Reconciliation)
- ☐ A Shared Likeness (Mediation)
- ☐ A Common Focus (Facilitation)

Remember! Abandonment, neglect, and abuse cause alienation in purposeful interdependent relationships. God does not impose His will upon us. Through His Holy Word, He reveals His desire to be very present and active in our lives. His only desire is that we embrace His presence.

"Here I am! I stand at the door and knock. If anyone hears my voice and opens the door, I will come in and eat with him, and he with me" (Revelation 3:20 NIV).

Share in God's Divine Order for your life and relationships. Allow Him to be your Master. Move on to discovering your created purpose on earth! What an opportunity! What an adventure!

Sensations of My Heart – Well Done

You may never sport myriad credentials behind your name.
You may never be inducted into the world's greatest Halls of Fame.

There may be some to count you out when the finish is too close to call.
At times, you may be weary; nevertheless, make no apologies for given your all.

Can These Bones Live?

There is one who knows all about you and how far you've really come.
He knows how you hung in there when hanging in there was no fun.

Dare not measure your life's worth by the sundry of things in which you possess.
Things are just things… nothing more and nothing less.

Life is a race we must all diligently run.

The greatest reward of all rewards is hearing the Master say," Well Done".

Choosing Your Mission

Can you remember saying to others, "When I grow up, I'm going to be a…"? Sometimes, choices are made for us. Inadvertently, we are left with the muddled task of cleaning up such choices.

When my father chose to leave our family, I was left to meander through boyhood and discover manhood without a man to guide me. So, I created this perfect world in my mind as a means of emotional survival. Instead of routinely playing with trucks and cars, I played house. Purposeful interdependent relationships became my passion. The absence of my father drove me to love hard and give unselfishly. I was on a mission to be a better man than my father was to me. Ideally, this was good. Developmentally, it was deficient. My definition of being better was only in comparison to what he wasn't. I felt like the world around me would be happy that I had such a commitment. One day while talking to God, He revealed the misdirection of my agenda. His agenda for me was to become a Godly Man, not just a good man! His intent was for me to represent Him in all walks of life. So, my mission became to glorify Him in all I do, wherever I go. I began the journey of becoming another "Man After God's Heart."

Do you have a clear understanding of your mission? Do you have a personal mission statement (See Workbook)?

Can These Bones Live?

Don't spend your time comparing yourself to others. Don't let others declare your success. Spend your time walking worthy of The Lord unto all pleasing, being productive in every good work, increasing in His knowledge, and growing in His grace.

Choosing Your Companion

Every person you allow in your space isn't committed to sharing your experiences. I have spent an enormous amount of time and energy seeking validation from the wrong people and trying to "fit in" the wrong places.

It is important to choose companions who "CARE." CARE is an acrostic that stands for: Compatible, Agile, Responsible, and Exponential.

Compatible
- ☐ Capable of being grafted, transfused, or transplanted from one individual to another without reaction or rejection.

Can These Bones Live?

Agile
- Positive, Practical, Productive

Responsible
- Able to be trusted to do what is right or to do the things that are expected or required

Exponential
- Operating in a greater power to a greater extent over time

Some of my fondest memories are the times I went fishing with my Uncle when he came home from the Army to visit. I was so excited about the prospect of catching fish. There were times I'd catch fish that didn't serve the greater purpose. My uncle would instruct me to throw it back or to release the fish that I'd caught. In my displeasure, I'd ask, "Why do I have to throw it back when I've waited so long to catch it?"

He replied, "it's too little to eat."

We were fishing for substance not for sport! I've come to consider this same principle when choosing

Can These Bones Live?

companions. There are times you must be willing to catch and release. Some relationships don't serve a greater purpose and are too small to keep.

The scripture says in Ecclesiastes 4:9-10 (NLT), *"Two people are better off than one, for they can help each other succeed. If one person falls, the other can reach out and help. But someone who falls alone is in real trouble."*

Are your chosen companions good for substance or just for sport? Are their aspirations too small for you to keep connected to your life's purpose? Do you need to release them?

When you make the right choices regarding your Master, Mission, and Companions, your adventures will be full of love, joy, and peace.

Can These Bones Live?

Chapter Two

CONNECT... DON'T COMPETE

Connection is the energy shared between two or more people which results in a shared likeness.

Connect

The process of connecting gives birth to us without destroying me!

We were created to connect and to accomplish greater purposes. Connection is the energy shared between two or more people which results in a shared likeness.

"Behold, how good and how pleasant it is For brethren to dwell together in unity! It is like the precious ointment…" (Psalms 133:1-2a KJV).

Competition is striving to gain or win something by defeating or establishing superiority over others who are trying to do the same thing.

The social and cultural trends of our day have made competition within relationships a norm.

Competition in the Social Arena

It's all about the game. In competition, you can only win at another's expense.

We see it in the election process when candidates try to establish superiority by minimizing their opponent's contributions, talents, or abilities. They often make promises that they can't keep. We see it in the world of sports as it displays the *thrill of victory* and *the agony of defeat*.

The rhetoric you hear from most companies is that they want to create a diverse, inclusive and highly competitive workforce. However, internal divides and self-serving behaviors stifle teamwork, growth, and productivity.

There seems to be much difficulty differentiating competition in the social arena (community, workplace) and competition in the sacred arena (family, friends).

Can These Bones Live?

Competition in the Sacred Arena

Family

The human family comes from one common stock. It is the most sacred of all earthly institutions.

"So God created man in his own image, in the image of God created he him; male and female created he them" (Genesis 1:27 KJV).

In a society where families are disoriented regarding their created purposes, there is only disintegration, destruction, and death. Ultimately, the society collapses.

Competition is manifested in the family through spousal spats, parental favoritism, and sibling rivalries.

Spousal Spats

Spousal Spats is the petty quarreling between spouse in an attempt to establish dominance or control over the other. You know... the fight to be right.

God created husbands and wives to cleave, not compete! To cleave is a two-fold process that establishes common form and function. It involves splitting or breaking away from preconceived ideas, pre-established behaviors and values and instead clinging or binding together with new ideas, behaviors, and values.

In many marriages today, both spouses work. The shared stress of balancing family and careers is constantly redefining the partnership roles. Often this stress lends itself to competition: who has the best job, who makes the most money, who's better known in the community, etc.

Society might have effectively redefined the method of "Playing the Game." However, it doesn't have the jurisdiction to change the sacred rules.

Can These Bones Live?

"For this reason a man will leave his father and mother and be united to his wife, and they will become one flesh" (Genesis 2:24 NIV).

Once man and woman understand and accept their purpose, they will see that it's not about superiority. It is about surrender and service. Each must surrender themselves to the will or authority of The Lord and serve one another as unto The Lord.

Parental Favoritism

Parental favoritism is the practice of giving unfair preferential treatment to one child at the expense of another. There are many reasons parents might favor one child over another. Here are a couple that I am familiar with.

Parents seemingly favor first and last born children over middle children. The firstborn and last born will have their parents all to themselves. This is not the case with middle children. They have to "grow up fast" and "get over it quick." Overall, it seems like the firstborn gets the most privileges and last born receive the most parental affection.

In mixed families, parents might favor their biological children over blended children.

Regardless to the nature of parental favoritism, the impacts are far more severe than any benefits the favored children get out of it (See Genesis 25:28-34). Isaac preferred Esau, while his wife preferred Jacob. The result was a divided home.

Children know when they are treated differently. It is hard for a child to reconcile how they feel with what is real. To make matters worse, parents are even more likely to play favorites once their children are grown up.

Sibling Rivalries

Sibling Rivalry is the display of jealousy among siblings with regards to talents, abilities, appearance and interests of other siblings. Jealousy and competition among siblings usually start at an early age as children try to gain their own identity and discover their own talents, abilities, and interests. Unfortunately, it often continues throughout adulthood when facilitated by parental favoritism.

Recently, I was on a motorcycle road trip to Key West, Florida. While enjoying dinner, one of the riders blurted out to two brothers who were sitting at the table enjoying one another, "Man I envy you guys. I see how you guys treat one another and wish I had that."

I could hear and see his brokenness as he shared how he and his siblings didn't get along. He went on to tell how he worked hard to earn money as a young boy. One of his siblings would say to him, "only a fool will work". However, on pay day, this sibling was the first to hold out a hand for money. If he didn't give the money, the sibling would try to forcefully take it. This, among other experiences, caused him to leave home at an early age.

He went on to have a successful career and retired from the automobile industry. Needless to say, his siblings had the same perspectives and engaged in the same behaviors. They try to make him feel guilty about his success and declare, "family is supposed to help each other". It is a major dysfunction in which abandonment, neglect, and abuse are common threads.

Friends

Friendships are primarily relationships of mutual trust supporting one another in mutual interests. When competition enters a friendship, the interest becomes self-serving. The narrative becomes comparative instead of collaborative.

Interdependent relationships are unique; however, they all must go through dynamic processes of forming and storming before they can function in a purposeful manner.

Forming

The Forming phase of interdependent relationships is a time when two or more people come together and gain a common knowledge of one another. It's a time to discuss and compare thoughts, principles, values, and goals. Many people *force* relationships rather than growing into them. In order to prohibit such social tragedy, individuals must be willing to form a genuine friendship.

The American Heritage Dictionary, Second College Edition, defines a friend as, "A person whom one knows, likes, and trusts."

During the forming phase of the relationship, it's important that each individual focus on becoming the type of person whom another would want to know, like, and trust.

Friendship is not about demands or controlling the interest of another. It's about comradeship, companionship, and communication. Each of these words began with "Com" which is Latin for together.

Comradeship literally means "together in the same chamber or room;" companionship literally means, "taking bread together;" communication literally means, "possessing together." This togetherness must possess a love that the Greek New Testament calls Phileo. Phileo is a cherishing love that expresses willful acceptance and respect for another.

We were created to connect and accomplish greater purposes. The process of connecting gives birth to "Us" without destroying "Me"!

Storming

No two independent forces can truly come together without experiencing this phase. It's like two independently large bodies of water coming together to form an even larger body. Each body of water has a unique composition. Each possesses great power; however, the process of tranquility can be rough.

The "Storming" phase of the relationship is one in which you are trying to balance expectations with behaviors. It's a time when many little idiosyncrasies surface. Perhaps these things were not evident during the "Forming" phase and you say to yourself, "I didn't see this side of him or her earlier". This connectivity requires proper alignment between expectations and behavior.

There are four distinguishable forces at work when describing the interconnection of expectations and behaviors. They are Proactive Engagement, Reactive Engagement, Reactive Disengagement and Proactive Disengagement (See Workbook).

Proactive Engagement

Proactive Engagement is when you know what is required and without prompt or pretense, do what is required because it's the right thing to do. This unconditional behavior is perhaps the greatest demonstration of personal ownership in interdependent relationships.

Reactive Engagement

Reactive Engagement is when you know what is required but you are waiting to see how the other person behaves before to commit to doing what's right. It's the kind of behavior that says "I'm not going to give or do any more than you are". Reactive Engagement is a form of neglect!

Reactive Disengagement

Reactive Disengagement is when you know what is required but refuse to communicate or collaborate because someone has offended you or hurt your feelings. Reactive Disengagement is a form of abandonment!

Proactive Disengagement

Proactive Disengagement is when you know what is required but purposefully behave in ways intended to manipulate and control people, situations and events. Proactive Disengagement is a form of abuse!

You must be acutely aware of the impact your behavior (what you do and how you do it) has on your interdependent relationship. Does your behavior create or calm the storm?

"Trust in the Lord with all your heart; do not depend on your own understanding. Seek his will in all you do, Don't be impressed with your own wisdom. Instead, fear the Lord and turn away from evil. Then you will have healing for your body and strength for your bones" (Proverbs 3:5-6 NLT).

Now that I've shared the foundation and developmental stages of interdependent relationships, let's add some ligaments to these bones.

Chapter Three

WHERE ARE THE B-O-N-E-S?

The things omitted are often deadlier than errors committed.

Where Are The B-O-N-E-S?

As conduits from Heaven to earth, we must be willing to allow the manifold graces of God to flow through us ...

The typical human skeletal system serves five major purposes: Support, Protection, Movement, Blood Cell Reproduction, and Mineral Storage. An unhealthy or dysfunctional skeletal structure results in an unhealthy or dysfunction body.

B-O-N-E-S is an acrostic for Blessings, Oneness, Nurturing, Edifying, and Sacrifice. Much like the human skeletal system, Blessings, Oneness, Nurturing, Edifying, and Sacrifice are the foundation for a healthy interdependent relationship.

Blessings

Tangible works of art fade with time; the passing trends may discredit them. However, blessings last forever! We manifest blessings through words and behavior. The New Testament word "Blessing" comes from two Greek words: eu, meaning, "well" and logos, meaning, "word." To bless is to speak a well word to and about others. Thus, it's important to realize the power of the tongue. The tongue can bring life or death to your relationships.

To bless is not an emotional decision governed by circumstances or situations. To bless is to take full responsibility for what you say or do as well as to take full ownership of the motive for what you say or do. The words of Solomon in Proverbs 8:6-8, clearly illuminate such responsibility when it says, "Hear; for I will speak of excellent things; and the opening of my lips shall be right things. For my mouth shall speak truth; and wickedness is an abomination to my lips. All the words of my mouth are in righteousness; there is nothing forward or perverse in them."

We must not look at blessings as a single or occasional act. We must see them as a willful response to every opportunity to speak or act well on behalf of others.

Can These Bones Live?

The "*Can These Bones Live?*" Workbook, highlights four "B's to Blessings (Be Prayerful, Be Kind, Be Thankful and Be Patient).

- ☐ **Be Prayerful** - Effectual prayers create an inseparable bond.

- ☐ **Be Kind** - A kind man benefits himself, but a cruel man brings trouble on himself."

- ☐ **Be Thankful** – When you truly value those you are in a relationship with, thankfulness erupts like lava from a volcano.

- ☐ **Be Patient** - Patience allows you to endure challenging people, situations, and circumstances for long periods of time without reacting in an irrational manner.

We are blessed by God to bless others. As conduits from Heaven to earth, we must be willing to allow the manifold graces of God to flow through us and reach those with whom we share time and space.

Oneness

Oneness requires a paradigm shift from viewing things in the plural tense to viewing things in a collaborative singular tense. You must not see interdependence as a compromise of your individualism; however, see it as a compliment. Evaluate all relationships whether familial, social, or professional. Do they complement you and your life's purpose? Are you one in vision, core values, and aspirations?

"Do nothing out of selfish ambition or vain conceit, but in humility consider others better than yourselves. Each of you should look not only to your own interests, but also to the interests of others" (Philippians 2:3-4 NIV).

I recall talking to a young woman who had recently gotten engaged. While being engaged provided her much joy, it also provided her much apprehension. She told me that the thing she feared most was losing her identity.

She was focusing on all of her accomplishments. She had a successful career. Her fiancée had a successful career. She didn't realize that they were in competition. They struggled over who made the most money and who had the finer things, etc. I explained

Can These Bones Live?

to her that she should not view it as a loss of identity. She should see it as a compliment to her identity.

I went on to tell her that if she wanted to succeed, it would take losing a self-centered identity and discovering a greater identity which gives birth to a life of shared purpose and meaning. This was essential to the growth and development of their interdependent relationship.

Two entities functioning as one unit can accomplish much more than either could alone. Oneness possesses the power to enlighten, to enrich, and to restore.

It's natural to nurture a relationship you value and to share in purpose as well as pursuit.

Nurturing

Nurturing is the attentive care given to keep a relationship thriving. Interdependent relationships are much like fine silver. Silver is quite beautiful and valuable; however, abandonment, neglect, or abuse can result in tarnish that's impossible to remove. Interdependent relationships require maintenance just as silver requires constant polishing and buffing in order to maintain its luster. While stainless steel may suffice, in no way does it compare in value to silver. If you want a high quality and high value relationship, you must be willing to take care of it. One shouldn't expect a relationship to increase in value if he or she doesn't invest the time necessary to care for it. The things omitted are often deadlier than errors committed. A state of "complacently good" is as much a threat to a purposeful relationship as is "consistently bad."

"Be devoted to one another in love. Honor one another above yourselves" (Romans 12:10 NIV).

The greatest lesson in nurturing is that of our Lord. In Matthew 20:28 KJV, He emphatically said, "He came not to be ministered unto but to minister." He literally meant that He came not to be served; however, He devoted His life to serving the needs of others.

Can These Bones Live?

Be devoted to the development of a purposeful interdependent relationship. Cherish the opportunities to share in greater experiences.

Edifying

Edifying is the deliberate attempts to build and not tear down. There is little more shattering and demeaning than casual "put downs." We have become so accustomed to dealing with them in our daily lives that we often fail to realize how devastating they can be in the long run. It's always bewildering when the people closest to you cause you the most pain. Could it be that individuals become so complacent with one another that they overlook the value that each brings into the relationship? Let's look at how the Bible addresses such a state:

"Let us therefore make every effort to do what leads to peace and to mutual edification" (Romans 14:19 NIV).

One thoughtless word or deed can destroy growth that took much effort and many years to accomplish. When Can These Bones Live?

people mutually bless and nurture one another, the results are edifying. They create a union that will withstand the trying times.

Sacrifice

Sacrifice is willingness to put the needs of others before your own comforts and conveniences. When friendship is the foundation for growing in interdependence, no sacrifice is too great.

"We do this by keeping our eyes on Jesus, the champion who initiates and perfects our faith. Because of the joy awaiting him, he endured the cross, disregarding its shame. Now he is seated in the place of honor beside God's throne. Think of all the hostility he endured from sinful people; then you won't become weary and give up" (Hebrews 12:2-3 NLT).

Jesus had an attitude of selfless service. He thought of Himself less and others more. He proved this by laying down His life for His friends (John 15:13). Self-sacrifice is not self-abasement. It's a willful choice to serve others in love. Sacrifice is about commitment not convenience. Sacrificial love is the truest expression of God.

Chapter Four

Bone of My Bone...

...The power of this submissive and sacrificial love is the catalyst to discovering a life full of joy and grace.

Bone of My Bone

The marriage process requires time, effort, sacrifice, and endless learning.

Former President George H.W. Bush stated while delivering a commencement speech in May 1992 at the University of Notre Dame, "Whatever form our most pressing problems may take, ultimately all are related to the disintegration of the family. If America is to resolve our social problems, we must first resolve our families."

According to *Enrichment Journal* on the Divorce Rate in America, the divorce rate in America for first marriages is 41 percent, second marriages is 60 percent and third marriages is 73 percent.

This startling statistic suggests that love alone is not enough to keep marriages together. Married people don't just grow apart; they fall into the relationship traps of abandonment, neglect, and abuse.

Can These Bones Live?

Destruction of Myth(s)

A successful marriage requires constant destruction of myths. We must attack and destroy them as quickly as television and other influences produce them.

"But at the beginning of creation God made them male and female. For this reason a man will leave his father and mother and be united to his wife, and the two will become one flesh. So they are no longer two, but one. Therefore what God has joined together, let man not separate" (Mark 10:6-9 NIV).

Marriage is no game wherein society decides on the participants and the rules. After God reviewed His creations and declared them good, He concluded that it was not good for the male to be alone. Man needed someone with common form and function. The operative word here is **common**. Man was given dominion over every beast of the field and every fowl of the air; however, there was no common form or function to share his life with. God realized that man needed friendship, fellowship, and intimacy from someone corresponding to himself; therefore, He uniquely created the woman.

"And Adam said, This is now bone of my bones, and flesh of my flesh: she shall be called Woman, because she was taken out of Man. Therefore shall a man leave his father and his mother, and shall cleave unto his wife: and they shall be one flesh. And they were both naked, the man and his wife, and were not ashamed" (Genesis 2:23-25).

The institute of marriage possesses a higher dignity and power. It's the first event God inaugurated into His plan for society. God chose the participants and established the rules.

One day filled with ceremonial bliss does not constitute marriage. It's only the beginning. The marriage process requires time, effort, sacrifice, and endless learning. Notice how I said, "the marriage process." A process is a series of actions, changes, and functions to bring about an end result. Processes generally consist of four fundamental components:

Inputs; Equipment/Tools; Knowledge/Skills; Outputs (See Workbook).

Remember, I told you earlier that I had created the perfect family in my head to survive the emotional trauma of childhood abandonment, neglect, and abuse. Needless to say, I had my ideals of marriage but was clueless as to the process. I just wanted a family of my own to give all that I didn't receive. I left my mother's house at the age of twenty and became a husband as well as a father to a three-year-old all at the same time. We spent years working on a marriage without working on the relationship. My prayers sounded more like, "Lord, fix my marriage" instead of, "Lord, fix me for my marriage."

Marriage is a triune institution in which God intends to mirror the interdependent relationship shared between Him and His Son (Divine Order), as well as, that of His Son and the church (Earthly Fulfillment). Both the New Testament and the Old Testament, compare God's relationship with His people to that of a bride and groom (Isaiah 61:11, Jeremiah 2:12, Revelation 21:2,9).

"But I would have you know, that the head of every man is Christ; and the head of the woman is the man; and the head of Christ is God" (1 Corinthians 11:3 KJV).

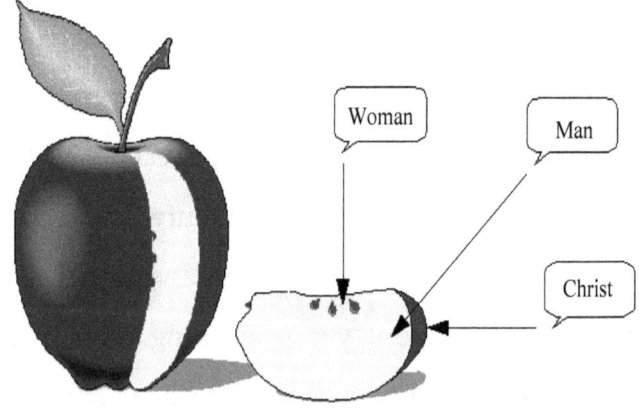

It's essential to realize God's Divine Order and to fulfill that order here on earth. I liken the fruitfulness of this order to an apple. After dissecting an apple, I received this awesome revelation.

The Apple – Symbolizes God who is the source of life. In Him is the fullness of all things.

Can These Bones Live?

The Peel - Symbolizes Christ. He is over the man. He protects the man and provides guidance, protection, and security for the marriage. With Jesus Christ as the head of the marriage, we have Divine providence. A marriage without Christ is incomplete and is subject to rapid deterioration as is the apple without a peel.

The Flesh - Symbolizes Man. He protects the woman by representing Christ's love for His church. Christ loved the church with a love that was:

- ☐ Constant
- ☐ Sacrificial
- ☐ Unconditional
- ☐ Understanding
- ☐ Unwarranted

The Core - Symbolizes the woman. She is the reproducer and supports man's existence. She is essential to all that man does and becomes.

When we section an apple, we refer to it as "a piece of an apple." This is an acknowledgment that the apple is no longer complete. The same applies with

Can These Bones Live?

marriage. A marital relationship is no longer complete when man and woman function independently of God's Divine Order.

Clearly, God's Order for your marriage is not about political correctness. It's about spiritual correctness. You must realize that God's Divine Order is not simply important, it should be the preeminent authority for all that you do.

A Message to the Man

God made you the head of woman not to dictate, to manipulate or to violate her. However, He has placed within your care a being and a body that gives greater meaning to your existence. You should humbly fulfill your responsibility to your wife and family. You represent Jesus Christ on earth. To represent is to "stand in for" or "bring back again." God has given you a precious gift (woman). You must bring God's Order back to your marriage by providing, protecting, and teaching in love (See Workbook).

Can These Bones Live?

A Message to the Woman

The Bible says in Proverbs 12:4 (KJV), "A virtuous woman is the crown to her husband: but she that maketh ashamed is rottenness in his bones".

Your spouse must be able to safely trust your integrity, ability and character to do him good and not evil. Consistently, show him that you respect his manhood as well as the virtues of womanhood. Avoid at all costs condescending languages and manipulative behaviors. Your responses to him are very important.

God created the first woman from man's rib. This authenticates interdependence. God made woman for the man; therefore, your person and purpose completes man.

Woman is like the seed of an apple. She substantiates life and fruitfulness. In Genesis, the second chapter, God referred to the woman as a helper. This does not mean she is inferior to man. The word helper more accurately means strength or power. Such strength and power are a compliment to man. Often God

Can These Bones Live?

himself is designated by the term Strength or Helper (Psalms 33:20).

God is well pleased when you grow in submissive and sacrificial love for your husband in order to help him fulfill his divine mandate to provide, protect and to teach in love. The power of this submissive and sacrificial love is the catalyst to discovering a life full of joy and grace.

You can unlock the doors of obscurity in your man's life.

As I stated earlier, in this chapter, the marriage process requires time, effort, sacrifice, and endless learning. My wife, Annie, and I, married late in life. There was much to learn as well as much to unlearn. Blending a family with adult children required much patience and understanding. Together, we were committed to destroying the marriage myths and fortifying our relationship by:

- ☐ Accepting one another without demanding
- ☐ Submitting to one another in "God Like" love

- ☐ Attacking our problems with resolution in mind
- ☐ Treating one another as gifts from God and not "good catches"
- ☐ Leading our blended family as one unit under God's authority

We hold His order as preeminent in our home, on our jobs and in our community. This experience supersedes any that either of us could have without the other. Our time together seems like eternity, while at the same time, as only one day. God made us uniquely perfect for one another.

Marriage is honorable!

Can These Bones Live?

Chapter Five

RECONCILING DIFFERENCES

...God is missing and they think we did it.

Can These Bones Live?

Reconciling Differences

An attempt to constantly define a problem and to determine its cause could become nothing more than "nagging" when you don't approach conflict with resolution in mind.

I recently attended a conference for United States Postal Service workers. One of the presenters was a Professor and taught communications at a local university. Interestingly, she said, "there are three basic responses to conflict: Peace Faking, Peace Breaking, and Peace Making. Hearing these terms led me to think further on the roles these basic responses play in reconciling differences in interdependent relationships.

Peace Faking

- ☐ Pretending (See Workbook).

Peace Breaking

- ☐ Offending (See Workbook).

Peace Making

- ☐ Mending

Healthy conflict resolution is a necessity if you are to have healthy interdependent relationships

Conflict is not always a bad thing. However, the mishandling of conflict is never a good thing.

"Work at getting along with each other and with God. Otherwise you'll never get so much as a glimpse of God." Hebrews 12:14 (The Message)

I am reminded of a story I once read on gatewaytojesus.com, which is an inspirational Christian connection website, with funny religious stories, clean church humor, amusing children stories and humorous bulletin bloopers. The story was about two little boys ages eight and ten, who were excessively mischievous. The two were always getting into trouble. Their parents could be assured that if any mischief occurred in their town, their two young sons were in some way involved.

The parents were at their wits end as to what to do about their sons' behavior. The mother had heard that a preacher in town had been successful in disciplining children in the past; therefore, she asked her husband if he thought they should send the boys to speak with the preacher.

The husband said, 'We might as well. We need to do something before I really lose my temper!' The preacher agreed to speak with the boys, but asked to see them individually. The 8-year-old went to meet with him first. The preacher sat the boy down and asked him sternly, 'Where is God?'

The boy made no response, so the preacher repeated the question in an even sterner tone, 'Where is God?' Again, the boy made no attempt to answer. So, the preacher raised his voice even more and shook his finger in the boy's face, 'WHERE IS GOD?'

Can These Bones Live?

Suddenly, the boy bolted from the room and ran directly home, slamming himself in the closet. His older brother followed him into the closet and asked what had happened. The younger brother replied, 'We are in BIG trouble this time. God is missing and they think we did it.'

Are you in "BIG trouble"? Is God missing in your behavior during the conflict resolution process?

Remember, God wants to reflect unselfish love and goodwill toward others through you. For this to happen, you must be willing to: Define the Problem, Determine the Causes, Decide Upon Solutions, and Do What You Decide.

Define the Problem

The Bible asks a very important question in Amos 3:3 NIV, "Do two walk together unless they have agreed to do so?" Does this mean that they will never encounter conflict? No! Does it mean that they will always share the same perspective? Certainly not! However, it's impossible to "walk together" unless there is a commitment to a shared purpose and direction. Reconciling differences is about "collaboration" or working together in a joint intellectual way.

To reconcile differences, you must be willing to define and communicate the problem based on facts not feelings (See Workbook).

You must not deal with generalities. Problem identification must be:

- ☐ Clear
- ☐ Concise
- ☐ Specific

Clear, concise, and specific problem definition can minimize the frustration associated with determining the causes of the problem.

Determine the Causes

Too often, we react to symptoms without determining the root cause of problems. When you look beyond the symptoms, you will find that the causes are either 'common' or 'special'.

Common cause problems are usually inherently woven into the fabric of one's personality or behavior and occur often. There must be a radical behavioral change in order to resolve conflict resulting from Common causes.

> Example: Bubba-Ray is spoiled and throws temper tantrums whenever he gets angry. He routinely blames others for his behavior. Everybody caters to him. Instead of confronting this common behavior, those around Him writes it off as special… you know, "that's just the way he is" or "he's just having a bad day" or "he's had a tough life". Bubba-Ray might be, "Special", but his behavior is not! Bubba-Ray needs a radical change that address his common selfish and undisciplined behavior. The temper tantrums are the symptoms, not the problem.

Can These Bones Live?

Special cause problems are those that occur occasionally. They are usually governed by situations and circumstances. It's important to understand such conflict. Special problems treated as though they are common will lead to exaggeration and overreaction.

> Example: Your best friend has had an unusually busy schedule this week. You are feeling neglected. You express as much; however, they ask you to understand the demanding schedule. You respond by saying, "You never have time for me." Never is the key word here. You have responded to a special situation that requires special attention as if it happens all the time. As a result, you overreact and perhaps create additional stress in the relationship.

Understanding the nature of the problem (i.e., common or special) can accelerate the resolution process.

Decide Upon Solutions

An attempt to constantly define a problem and to determine its cause could become nothing more than "nagging" when you don't approach conflict with resolution in mind. You must decide on solutions that are in the best interest of your relationship.

Forgiveness must be your initial solution to resolve any problem. We must be willing to forgive when offended and seek forgiveness when we are the offender. Jesus said in Matthew 6:15-14 NLT, "If you forgive those who sin against you, your heavenly Father will forgive you. But if you refuse to forgive others, your Father will not forgive your sins.

Often, I hear people say, "I will forgive, but I will not forget." The *American Heritage Dictionary, Second Edition*, defines forgiveness as, "passing over an offense and to freeing the offender from the consequences of it."

All of us have scars that have become a permanent part of us. Many have left scars that are a permanent part of others' lives. We can even recall the incidents that caused the scars. Nevertheless, we can choose not to recreate the pain and to rebuild the story every time we see the scar. This should be our attitude towards forgiveness. Look at the scar if you must but release the offender, relieve yourself of the pain and build a new story.

For me, this moment of truth came when my father announced that he was coming to Arkansas and that he wanted to see me. This was one of the few times in my entire life to see him. The very thought of this created conflict within me. I had told myself all these years that I was okay, when in reality, I was "Peace Faking." I wanted to somehow invoke my pain on him because he had hurt me. When I saw him, I hated the fact that I looked just like him. As I listened and watched him awkwardly try to make peace having not done more for my brother and me, it was obvious to me that he was in the early stages of dementia. A spirit of empathy overwhelmed me. I realized my love for him was much greater than my pain. I traded places with him and tried to view life from his vantage point.

He left our family when he was 21-years-old. A wife and two children is a lot to handle if you are not prepared. I was able to thank him for what he did do. I was able to make peace with myself and with him. After all, if it weren't for this experience, I wouldn't be the man I am today.

I've often heard that you can't miss something you never had; however, I beg to differ. I missed my father's active presence. Nevertheless, his missing in action taught me more than I've learned from any man. It taught me to be passionately active in all relationships. It taught me to put others before myself. For my children, I wanted to be the lovingly active father I never had. For my wife, I wanted to be the loving husband my mother never had. For my siblings, I wanted to be a brother that they could count on. For my friends and associates, I wanted to be someone they could genuinely like and trust.

My father passed away May 2014. I flew to Portland, Oregon to go to the funeral and to pay my respect. Due to a shortage in Pallbearers, I was unexpectedly asked

Can These Bones Live?

to assist in carrying His body into the church. There I was at the head of the coffin. It seemed like the heaviest burden I'd ever encountered. The weight of the world was seemingly on my shoulders as I struggled up three flights of stairs. Therein was a moment of acceptance. No father or mother should leave this world without their child honoring them however they can.

As I stood at the altar staring at this person I never knew, I realized his presence. I was sure that he was with me and that he knew I was there with him. Therein was a moment of peace. Our last words to one another were words of acceptance, love, and forgiveness.

While trying to wrap my head around what I was feeling, I was again unexpectedly asked to do one final thing. I was asked to give the benediction and to commit my father's body back to mother earth. Another moment came! Perhaps, it was just as painful for him as it was for me for us not to grow together. Tis the moment of greater revelation. Things aren't always as they seem.

Do What You Decide

Sensations of My Heart -- Fabricators

Speech smoother than oil; Talking just for the thrill.

Lips dripping with honey; Crocked by their own folly.

Saying they will when they really won't; Saying they do when they really don't.

Saying they can with no real intention; Why can't they just do what they mention?

Good intentions don't automatically lead to good results. You must follow up and follow through. Be a Primer mover. Be the force that initiates the process.

Can These Bones Live?

"Therefore, if you are offering your gift at the altar and there remember that your brother has something against you, leave your gift there in front of the altar. First go and be reconciled to your brother; then come and offer your gift" (Matthew 5:23-24 NIV).

Be a "Peace Maker"! Don't be a "Peace Breaker" by being punitive and uncooperative. Forgiveness isn't earned, it's graciously given. An unforgiving spirit is a lethal blow to conflict resolution.

The Apostle Paul highlighted the benefits of willful forgiveness when he said, "… when I forgive whatever needs to be forgiven, I do so with Christ's authority for your benefit, so that Satan will not outsmart us. For we are familiar with his evil schemes (II Corinthians 2:10-11 NLT).

- ☐ **Forgive for other's sake** …Lest they be overtaken by sorrow.
- ☐ **Forgive for Christ's sake**. We honor Christ when we forgive others as He has forgiven us.

Can These Bones Live?

- **Forgive for the relationship sake.** Don't let Satan break harmony and hijack your purposeful relationship.

Forgive with a compassionate heart and a clear conscious.

It's also worth mentioning that not only is forgiveness a necessary solution, the reestablishment of boundaries is also necessary. Boundaries are the "rules of engagement." They should be clear and agreed upon requirements for continuing your journey together.

Early in life I learned to suppress how I felt because I didn't want to say or do things that would hurt others. My response was to internalize my feelings and to emotionally escape. I found that in my "Peace Faking", I developed high expectations but low tolerance when it came to conflict. When I finally decided to face it, I found myself trying to deal with what happened every mile as I ran away from it. I eventually learned that I had to adjust my expectations without having to adjust my aspirations. From this, I've also learned not to burden one person or relationship with the responsibility of being everything to me. Sometimes we want people to behave in ways they haven't agreed to.

I hear you saying, "but what if things don't get better?"

Reconciliation doesn't always mean restoration. When attempting to reconcile, seek forgiveness or ask for forgiveness in private. If the person or persons reject your efforts, seek mediation from an unbiased person who's qualified to assist with conflict management. If the person still rejects your efforts to reconcile, release them. Accept that it is not your job to change the person; it's your job to forgive the person. Perhaps, that fish is too small to keep!

Conflict doesn't have to destroy your purposeful interdependent relationships. Reconciling differences is a natural sweetener that will facilitate unspeakable joy.

Chapter Six

MAINTAINING INTERDEPENDENT RELATIONSHIPS

An effectively maintained interdependent relationship is like a well-balanced triangle.

Maintaining Interdependent Relationships

In Ezekiel 37, the whole house of Israel's hope was gone. They were cut off from the hydration and sweetness of God's grace. They had failed to nurture and to edify their interdependent relationship with The Sovereign Lord. Consequently, they could not respond to nor benefit from His everlasting love, peace, and joy. There was no communication, there was no passion, and there was no intimacy.

An effectively maintained interdependent relationship is like a well-balanced triangle. Each side represents an indispensable ingredient. Communication is the base of the triangle. Intimacy is the left side. Passion is the right side (See Workbook).

Communication

A priceless jewel to any interdependent relationship is effective communication skills. Communication is a combination of clear delivery of speech and actively listening (See Workbook). The main objective for communication should always be to get an understanding. Clear speech and actively listening quickens the spirit and brings life to the conversation.

The Nation of Israel's bones didn't bolster; neither did their tendons and flesh take form until they actively listened to the clear delivery of speech from the Prophet Ezekiel.

Actively listening and being physically present when someone is talking to you are not synonymous. While you might not always enjoy what another person says, you must give that person the grace of being heard. People generally know when they are talking at you and not to you. You can expedite a person's willingness to trust you when you show that you are interested in what they are saying.

It's important that you don't judge or criticize what the speaker is saying. You can disagree with what the other person says without judgment or criticism. Criticism prohibits open communication.

Can These Bones Live?

Extend the grace of being heard! It can help generate passion.

Passion

Passion is boundless enthusiasm that creates momentum towards a purpose or goal. When I think of passion, I think of how honeybees behave while making honey. All honeybees are social and cooperative insects. While there are three classes of bees in the colony, they work in concert to complete the complex task of gathering nectar and sweet deposits from plants and building and protecting the hive as well as modifying and storing the deposits in the honeycomb. If a queen bee dies, the worker bees select another queen and feed it a special diet until it becomes fertile. The honey becomes a source of food and sustains the bees during the winter months when there are no plants from which to draw nectar.

Like the honeybees, you must:

- ☐ Recognize life's many sources of healthy deposits that can lend to a purposeful interdependent relationship.
- ☐ Become responsible for producing and storing sweetness in your familial, social, and professional relationships with boundless enthusiasm.
- ☐ Become creative in extracting and expressing all that you've stored for the good of others
- ☐ If one source of fulfillment in your relationships dies, select another and nourish it to fertility.

Effective communication and passion will produce intimacy.

Intimacy

Most people when hearing the word intimacy tend to think of romantic relations. However, simply put, intimacy is the closeness of observation or knowledge of a subject.

Sensations of My Heart -- Count on Me

When you are weak, for us I will be strong.

When you are slipping, I will help you hold on.

When you are down, I will be there to pick you up.

When you are thirsty, drink from my cup.

When you are overwhelmed, have no fear.

You can count on me; I am always here.

Intimacy says, because I observed you and know you, I care about you. All relationships must experience intimacy if they are to grow in purpose. People tend to become more transparent when they know they are accepted for who they are.

The bible says, in Mark 9:50 (NLT), "Salt is good for seasoning. But if it loses its flavor, how do you make it

Can These Bones Live?

salty again? You must have the qualities of salt among yourselves and live in peace with each other."

Salt is a mineral that has been used since ancient times in many cultures. The Bible contains numerous references to salt. In various contexts, it is used metaphorically to signify: Permanence, Loyalty, Durability, Fidelity, Usefulness, Value and Purification.

Communication, passion and intimacy is the nectar and sweet deposits for a well-balanced interdependent relationship. Like salt, they must flavor the relationship with: Permanence, Loyalty, Durability, Fidelity, Usefulness, Value and Purification.

With each new day, comes new opportunities.
- ☐ The Courageous embrace them and live!
- ☐ The Complacent ignore them and simply exist!
- ☐ The Cowardly dries up and dies!

Can These Bones Live?

Conclusion

Every interdependent relationship goes through a continuous cycle of excitement, frustration, and indecision.

There is no one answer for the disintegration of meaningful relationships. Every situation is different. Nonetheless, Satan is yet using deception as a main tool. This tool lures us into the forbidden fruit of selfishness. It's time to turn a deaf ear to him. Let him know that he will not wreak havoc in your relationships.

Many times, we want to see better results in our lives; nevertheless, we are not willing to become what we need to become to produce those results. If what you are doing is "good," don't assume everything is "fine."

Relationships require continuous education as well as continuous improvement. One shouldn't think that love is all he or she needs. Just as you learn to love an individual, you must also learn to live and to function with them interdependently. Interdependence is not abandonment of individuality. It's the entwinement of two individuals in order to experience the joy of sharing one love, one life, and one legacy.

Life is truly an adventure!

It's important that you have the proper guidance when considering the path you take. Who better to guide you than The One who created you and knows all about you? You don't have to live beneath your God appointed privilege. Take control of your interdependent relationships by adhering to God's Order. Live to fulfill His Divine purpose in you.

Remember, in order to grow with a person, you must first know, like, and trust them.

Such knowledge will facilitate a friendship that produces an unshakeable foundation for growth and greater meaning. Should your friendship grow into a companionate love affair, you must cleave to the object of your love and leave any influence that is not in the best interest of your relationship. Competition has no place in growing together unless you are competing to make love full and complete. The objective is not to keep score but to keep scoring! Give all you have for the good of your relationship. Allow the principles and doctrines of Christ to guide you along the way.

"Through thy precepts I get understanding: therefore, I hate every false way. Thy word is a lamp unto my feet, and a light unto my path" (Psalms 119:104-105 KJV).

It's unrealistic to think your relationship will never encounter conflict. Nonetheless, how you handle conflict is most important. You must be willing to immediately resolve conflict and to reconcile your differences in a spirit of love and meekness. Every trial you encounter is not meant to break the harmony within your relationship. Conflict can teach you how to love in a greater way if you choose to use it in that manner. Be willing to forgive. Freely turn away from evil, and hold on to the good.

Every interdependent relationship goes through a continuous cycle of excitement, frustration, and indecision.

Don't allow your relationship to become brittle, bleached, and broken due to the heated pressures of life. Through steadfast commitment, passion, and intimacy, you can maintain a growing and fulfilling relationship.

If you are thinking, "That all sounds good" ... you should try it! It is that good!

Sensations of My Heart -- Finally

... You've taken flight in my soul as ten-thousand startled pheasants.
I'm staggered by your power and am enthralled by your presence.
Should you... Would you... Could you possibly be?
Time and time again; I thought you'd never return to me.

Can These Bones Live?

I've longed for you since childhood.

I vividly tend to remember.

... the countless hours spent dreaming of and pantomiming our lives together.

I'm not the same as I was then; have grown tremendously.

I understand you better and appreciate you more.

True Life... Finally

God intends for you to experience love, joy, and peace while sharing your life with another. He intends for you to discover purposes much greater than your own. When you apply principles outlined in this book, you will have "the right things happening, the right way" and will experience joy unspeakable and full of His glory.

May His richest blessings become yours as you grow into vessels of honor... fit and conditioned for the Master's use... prepared unto every good work.

Your Bones Can Live!

All His Best,

About the Author

Ricky Allen is the Founder, Bishop and Sr. Pastor of the Immanuel Family Worship Center, Incorporated of Jacksonville, Arkansas. He is a Visionary anointed for Kingdom Leadership!

An extraordinary communicator and motivator, the author's passion for ministry and meaningful relationships are apparent as he leads, teaches and counsels.

He is married to Annie Jean Allen. They have five children.

Acclaim for 'Can These Bones Live?'

*I have known Bishop Ricky Allen since he was a 16-year-old lad. He has always shown great leadership skills, high intelligence, integrity and a sincere love for Jesus Christ. I'm very happy to call Bishop Allen my friend. He is the kind of friend you know will be there if you need someone to talk to, or if you were in real trouble.
Congratulations on your new book,
and for making a difference in our community.*
~ ***Charles D. Stuart/Little Rock, AR***

Bishop Ricky Allen speaks with clarity the value of a nurturing environment for relationship growth. He asserts that relationships don't die a natural death. Can These Bones Live presents a pathway leading to better interdependent relationships.
~ **DR. Lou J Turner/Jacksonville, AR**

*Wow! Profound! Calm! Surprising! Fantastic!
Ricky Allen's new life-help book is deeply personal, honest, and will provoke you to action. The author expertly guides you to a promised enlightenment!*
~**Iris M. Williams/Little Rock, AR**

Can These Bones Live? *gives us a framework for forming and sustaining relationships that demonstrate the mystery of God's grace in spite of the corrosive, cultural forces of society. Now more than ever, there is a need for clear and sound teaching on building healthy, God-centered relationships. And, Bishop Allen is a tested, trust-worthy, and true vessel to proclaim what Christ has taught on this matter. As a son in pursuit of Christ, I have grown to appreciate Bishop Allen's stewardship of God's calling, and it is my earnest prayer that the invisible, living God will become visible and palpable by all who read this work.*
~David Ford, Alexandria, VA

Coming Soon:

Beneath the Sun

**What happens
when you find a love you're
destined to have,
but it doesn't look like the
established norms?**

Redo Stuart and Beatrice Napal are two 'unlikely' individuals who found 'unlikely' love in an 'unlikely' place – right where they were!

On an African tour, the two meet and experience an instant connection. "It's as if all of my childhood dreams have all come true in you," Beatrice admits.

"Unlike most boys, I didn't play with cars and trucks. I played house. I dreamed of love and a family that I could love and who would love me back," Redo confesses.

PROLOGUE

It's 6:00 AM, Monday Morning at the Le Royal Mansour. I hear the birds singing. As I slowly drag out of bed due to the long flight and sleepless night, I am drawn to the light piercing through my window.

I make a fresh cup of coffee and walk out onto my balcony. I am taken by the beauty of butterflies glistening in the sun as they gently land upon the Roses of Sharon in the well-manicured indoor courtyard.

Is this just a prolusion to what awaits me ... great cities, vast deserts and picturesque coastlines? I've got twelve days to soak it all in.

I purposed for this trip to be one of relaxation from my busy life back in the States. As a single professional, working for a Fortune 500 Corporation and a clergyman with pastoral duties, seldom have I taken time for just me. For once, I was alone and had nothing and no one to serve but me.

It would be a time for me to re-center and reconnect.

Twelve Days! Seven Different Places!

I had no idea that I would experience moments that would change my life…

ONE

Nowhere To Be

Casablanca [kas-uh-blang-kuh]

What a way to start a day. The birds are singing, butterflies are flying, and I have nowhere to be and plenty of time to get there.

My original plan was to get up, rent a car and freelance. However, I quickly realized that there was so much to see, and I didn't know where to start. I went down for breakfast and indulged in my favorite (pancakes, scrambled eggs with cheese, hash browns, coffee and a small glass of ruby red grapefruit juice). After breakfast, I decided to walk it off. I stopped by the concierge desk to commandeer a map.

"Hello, Victor!"

"Hello Mr. Stuart," Victor the concierge replied. "How did you sleep?"

"Like a rock," I replied.

Victor laughed and said with a French accent, "I didn't know rocks slept."

"They don't," I said. "They sink. And, that's exactly what I did. When my head hit that pillow, I sank into unconsciousness." We both laughed.

"What are your plans for the day, Mr. Stuart?"

"Victor, you can call me Redo."

"Merci beaucoup, Monsieur Redo."

"You are welcome," I said.

I knew very little French and wasn't brave enough to respond in French.

"What are my plans for the day? Well, Victor, I thought I would walk around a bit, rent a car and do a little driving."

"Is this your first trip to Morocco," he asked. "What brings you here?"

"Yes, it is my first trip to Morocco," I told him. "Morocco just sounded like fun! I wanted to experience a different culture."

"Monsieur Redo might I suggest a full tour of the Moroccan region? I have a guided tour with one more open slot. The bus leaves at 12:00 noon. I can get you on it; if you are flexible."

"Victor," I said fully intrigued. "I've got twelve days to flex, tell me more…"

Casablanca is the largest city in Morocco. It is the very thing I was trying to escape. I desired a more quiet and intimate setting to unwind and relax. However, I was looking forward to exploring what the city had to offer. The brochure Victor gave me did an excellent job of painting an appealing picture.

Soon it was noon and time for me to board the tour bus. I hated to leave the comforts of the Le Royal Mansour and the gentle breeze from the Atlantic Ocean. However, I was excited as I boarded the 25-passenger tour bus.

As we rode through the whitewashed Moorish buildings that extended from the coast, I appreciated the stimulating mixture of tower blocks and French colonial architecture. I slowly began to unwind and embrace the tour.

Pierre, the tour guide explained, "The itinerary for the day is a visit to Hassan II Mosque and the local souqs."

I hadn't done much research on Morocco and didn't have a clue as to what to expect. Regardless, I was entirely open to adventure and discovery.

The Hassan II Mosque was one of just two mosques in the country that's open to non-Muslims. The mosaics, marble columns, horseshoe-shaped arches and carved, painted wooden ceilings are breathtaking.

I find the souqs (marketplaces) interesting. The canvas of local food, handicrafts from leather bags to brightly painted pottery and giant bowls of olives are intense. Trading caravans gathered and sold their goods here. Not only are they marketplaces, but they also serve as cultural centers for many celebrations and festivals.

The vibrant colors of people, buildings and merchandise are so atmospheric.

TWO

A Piece Of Heaven

Rabat [rah-baht]

The moonlit fifty-seven-mile drive along the Northern Atlantic coast was spectacular! It's 7:00 PM. I could smell citrus as we drove through the orange groves in route to the Villa Mandarine Hotel. It's been a long day. I'm ready for bed.

"Good evening Monsieur," the front desk clerk greeted me as I approached him.

"Good evening," I replied.

"May I have your name please?"

"Redo Stuart."

"We have your room ready Monsieur Stuart."

"Thank you," I responded returning his friendly smile. "I'm ready for my room."

"Our rooms feature a seating area with an LCD TV as well as a private balcony with views of the garden," he explained. "Here you are he said. Room 913. The elevators are down the hall to the left."

I grabbed my bags, and up to the room, I went.

I swiped the key, but as a long day would have it, the door failed to unlock. I tried a second and third time. Still, the door wouldn't open.

Back to the lobby, I go.

"How's your room, Monsieur Stuart?"

"Well, I don't know," I managed to remain calm. After all, it wasn't his fault. "My key wouldn't work."

"My apologies," he said with genuine concern.

Suddenly she appeared and stood as still as the sun while everything in the lobby seemingly rotated on its axis. Taken by her graceful stride, I went deaf for a moment.

"Monsieur, Monsieur," I heard him calling to me. "Your new key."

"I'm sorry," I offered.

"No problem," he said as he grinned and handed me my new key.

This time I was able to access my room. The room was nicely appointed. Its contemporary styling was a canvas of white with accents of lemon yellow, lime green. It was a pleasant compliment to the spa-like surroundings.

The next morning, after coffee on the balcony, I went down for breakfast on the terrace which led onto the gardens.

Man, this is great I thought. But that thought was quickly replaced by the ideals of being successful and single. If I could count the times I've heard, "you need a woman" and charge a dollar each time I've listened to that, I'd have enough to buy that new motorcycle, I've been saving to purchase.

I'm single by choice. I am preparing for that woman God has arranged for me. Members of "match makers anonymous" mainly family and friends, just don't know when to stop.

Today is a free day. Pierre, the tour guide, informed us that Rabat was not in the main lineup of Morocco's tourist attractions. However, he said this Capital City was full of charm. The international flair and importance signify the presence of foreign embassies and dignitaries. The palm tree-lined boulevards are clean and relatively free of traffic. This is a welcomed relief from the hustle and bustle of Casablanca. It is a suitable day for walking.

Among the many exciting things to do, I decided to spend the day at Museum Mohamed VI of Modern and Contemporary Art. The vibrant paintings and eccentric statues were aspiring. I must say the Picasso and Out of Africa exhibits were among my favorites. As I continued to revel in such creative genius, I notice something strikingly familiar. It was her!

She seemed just to appear.

There she was standing and gazing intensely at the art and writing something in a leather bonded legal pad.

Lost in a mental wonderland of inquiry, I drew closer to her.

Who was she? Where did she come from? Even more, what was she writing?

Is it me? Or is this divine? Is it real or just an aspect of my mind? Does destiny find us at such a place, at such a time? Why am I thinking in ways I've never thought?

Why am I feeling things I've never felt? Could I have been Adam and she had been Eve? What is it about her that foments my curiosity?

She was deeply engrossed in this particular piece of art and never saw me coming. It was an exquisite rendition of the sun with its 'bronze orange' rim surrounding various geometric shapes of all sizes and vibrant colors, neatly grouped in what appeared to be regions with transparent boundaries.

"Excuse me," I said to her.

She jumped as though she had touched an unnoticeable hot flame and grabbed her chest as if her heart was trying to escape.

"I'm sorry," I quickly apologized and extended my hand. "I didn't mean to startle you. I couldn't help but notice you and your appreciation for this piece of art. Redo Stuart."

"Beatrice Napal," she recovers and offers her hand to meet mine.

Something leaped inside me like ten-thousand startled pheasants springing up from the bushes of a hunted field.

I felt alive!

It was a piece of heaven.